Why Does This Float?

Written by Ben Smith

Matter

Vital Vocabulary

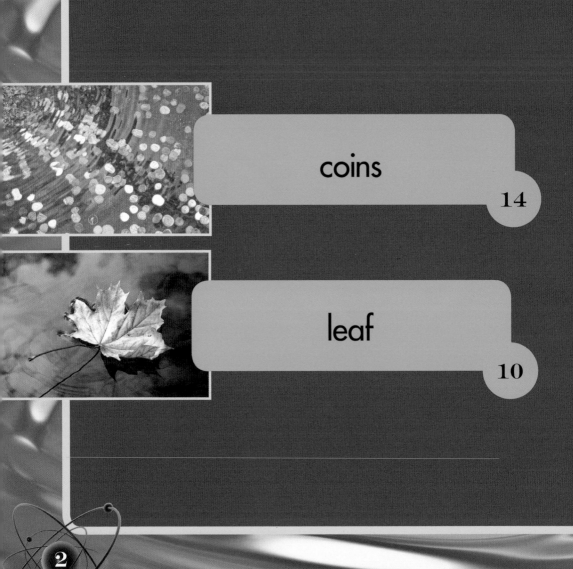

2

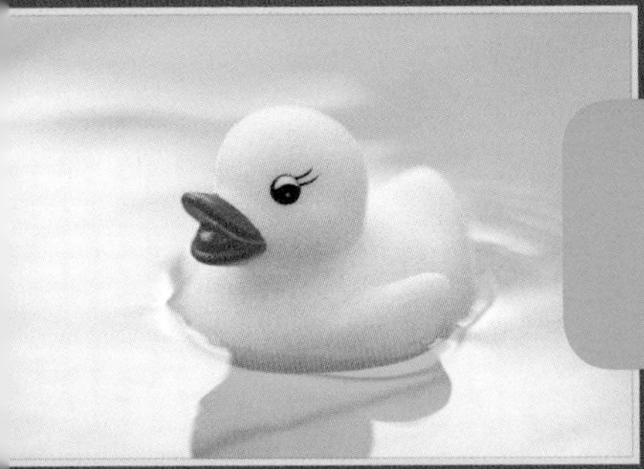

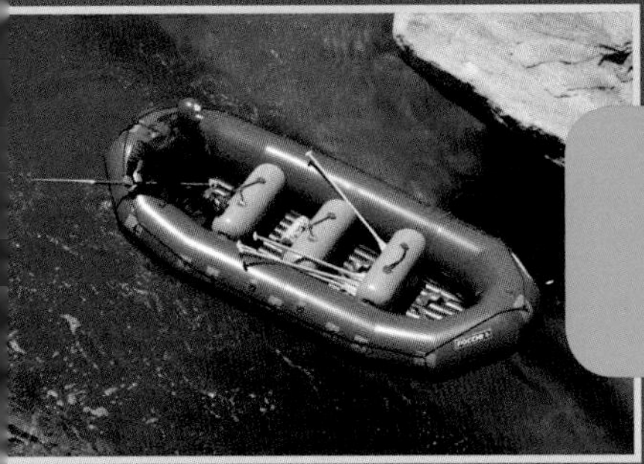

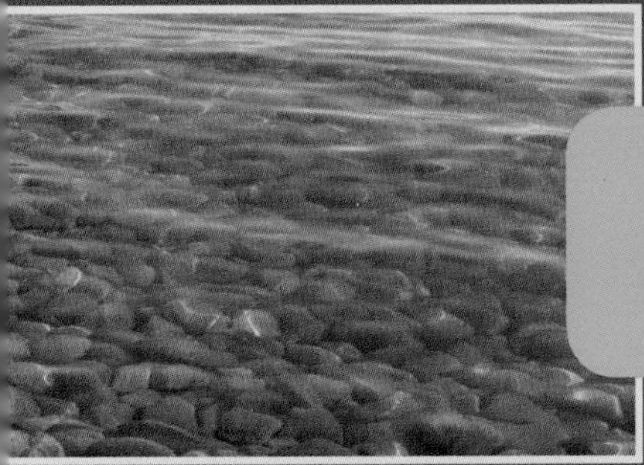

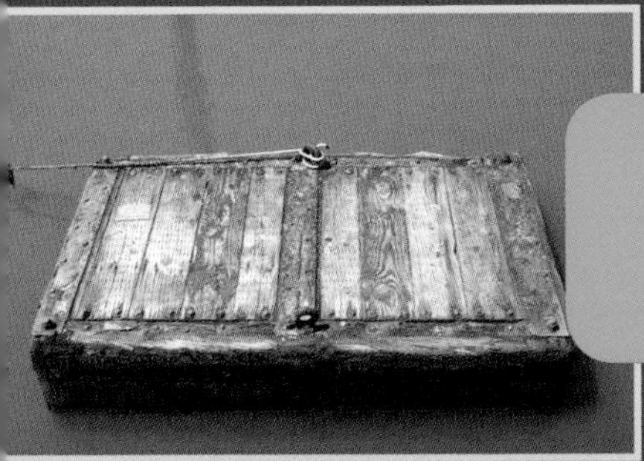

This duck is made of plastic.
Plastic is lighter than water.
So the duck floats.

This plastic duck
is very light.

This raft is made of wood.
Wood is lighter than water.
So the raft floats.

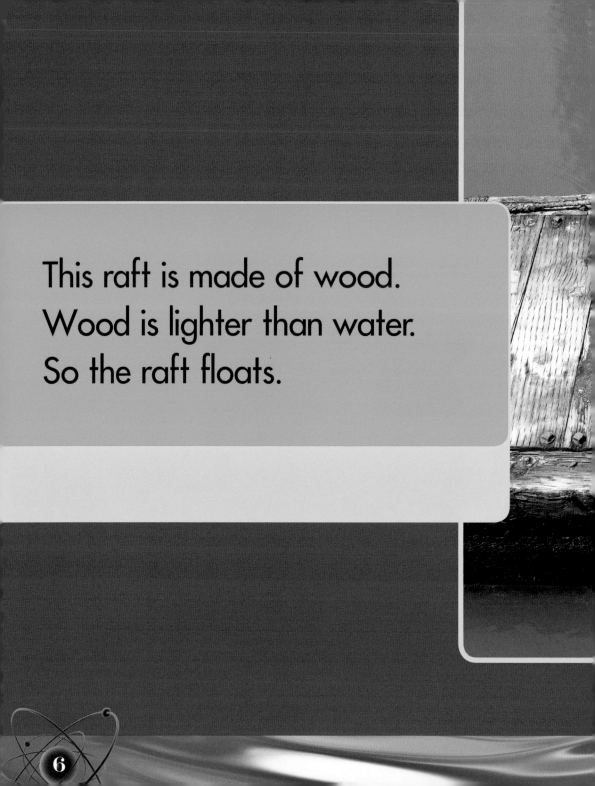

You can stand on
this wooden raft.

This boat is made of rubber.
Rubber is lighter than water.
So the boat floats.

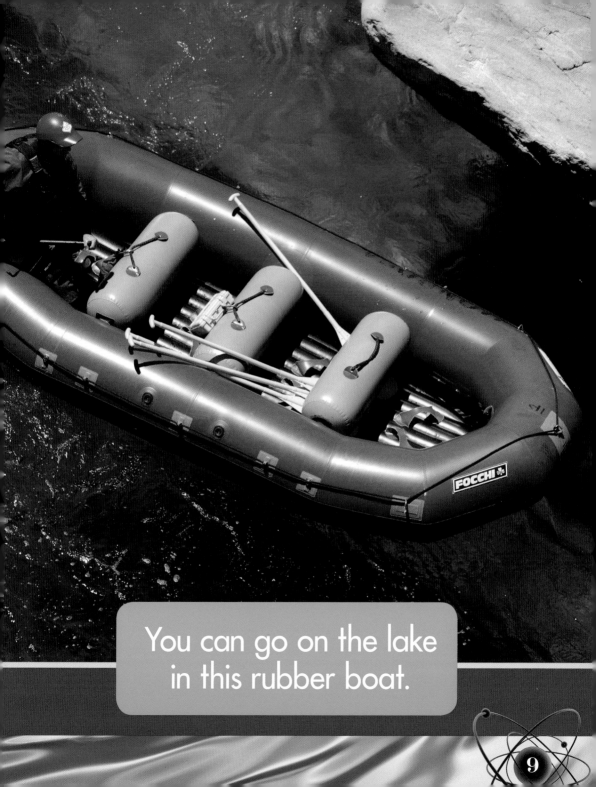

You can go on the lake
in this rubber boat.

This is a dry leaf.
A dry leaf is lighter than water.
So the leaf floats.

A dry leaf is
very light.

The leaf got wet.
It got wet in the water.
The water made it heavy.
So it sank.

This leaf has sunk to the bottom of a pond.

stones

coins

Stones and coins
are heavier than water.
So they sink.

Object	Sink	Float
plastic duck	no	yes
wooden raft	no	yes
rubber boat	no	yes
dry leaf	no	yes
wet leaf	yes	no
stones	yes	no
coins	yes	no

Critical Thinking

Find out what these things are.
Put them in water.
Find out if they sink or float.